Tuba

EASY CLASSICS

arranged for brass quintet
by Charles Sayre

easy level

THE CANADIAN
BRASS

CANADIAN
BRASS
SERIES OF
COLLECTED QUINTETS

TWO CHORALES

1. O Sacred Head

TUBA

J. S. Bach
(1685-1750)
arranged by Charles Sayre

Legato tongue throughout unless otherwise slurred.

2. Break Forth, O Beauteous Heavenly Light

TWO FUGUING TUNES

1. When Jesus Wept

TUBA

*Legato throughout

2. Kittery

VICTORIOUS LOVE
(Amor Vittorioso)

TUBA

Giovanni Giacomo Gastoldi
(c1550- c1622)
arranged by Charles Sayre

Play through the piece twice.

IN THE HALL OF THE MOUNTAIN KING

TUBA

Edvard Grieg
(1843-1907)
arranged by Charles Sayre

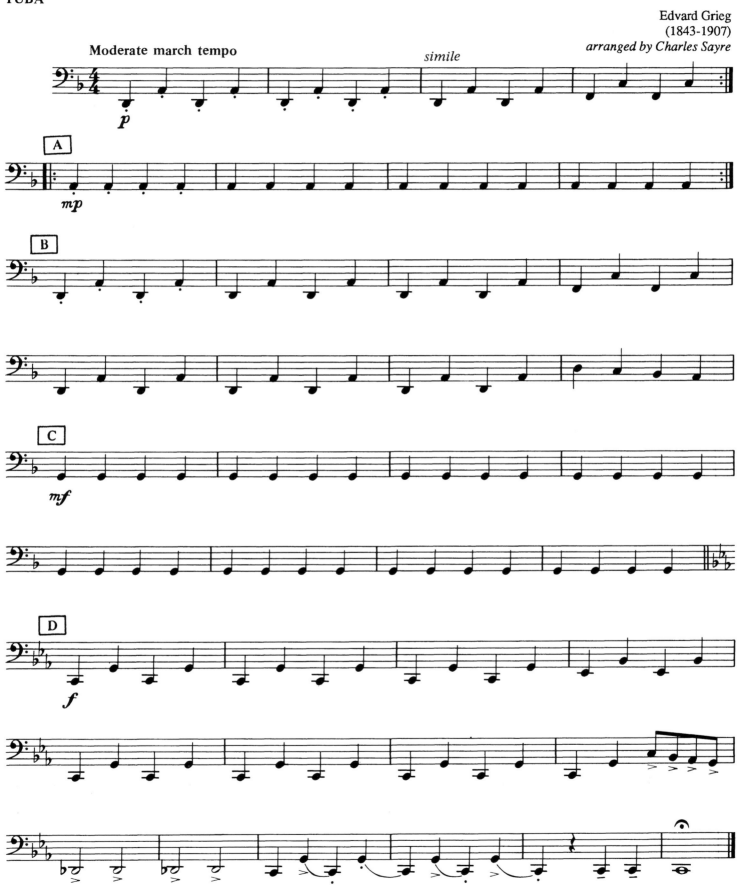

AUSTRIAN HYMN

TUBA

Franz Joseph Haydn
(1732-1809)
arranged by Charles Sayre

CANON

TUBA

Thomas Tallis
(c1505-1585)
arranged by Charles Sayre

C A N A D I A N   B R A S S

SERIES OF
COLLECTED QUINTETS

EASY CLASSICS

arranged for brass quintet
by Charles Sayre

contents

2	J. S. Bach	Two Chorales
		O Sacred Head
		Break Forth, O Beauteous Heavenly Light
3	William Billings	Two Fuguing Tunes
		When Jesus Wept
		Kittery
4	Giovanni Giacomo Gastoldi	Victorious Love
5	Edvard Grieg	In the Hall of the Mountain King
6	Franz Joseph Haydn	Austrian Hymn
7	Thomas Tallis	Canon

Welcome to the new *Canadian Brass Series of Collected Quintets*. In our work with students we have for some time been aware of the need for more brass quintet music at easy and intermediate levels of difficulty. We are continually observing a kind of "Renaissance" in brass music, not only in audience responses to our quintet, but to all brass music in general. The brass quintet, as a chamber ensemble, seems to have become as standard a chamber combination as a string quartet. That could not have been said twenty-five years ago. Brass quintets are popping up everywhere — professional quintets, junior and senior high school ensembles, college and university groups, and amateur quintets of adult players.

We have carefully chosen the literature for these collected quintets, and closely supervised the arrangements. Our aim was to retain a Canadian Brass flavor to each arrangement, and create attractive repertory designed so that any brass quintet can play it with satisfying results. We've often remarked to one another that we certainly wish that we'd had quintet arrangements like these when we were students!

Happy playing to you and your quintet.

THE CANADIAN BRASS

U.S. $7.99

ISBN-13: 978-1-4584-0152-6

Distributed By
HAL LEONARD

0 73999 80224 5

HL50488764

50488764   9 781458 401526

HAL•LEONARD®
CORPORATION

7777 W. BLUEMOUND RD. P.O. BOX 13819 MILWAUKEE, WI 53213